CANADIAN HISTORY TIMELINES

North-West Restistance

Blaine Wiseman

Weigl

Published by Weigl Educational Publishers Limited
6325 – 10 Street SE
Calgary, Alberta, Canada
T2H 2Z9

Website: www.weigl.ca

Library and Archives Canada Cataloguing in Publication data available upon request.
ISBN 978-1-77071-283-6 (hardcover)
ISBN 978-1-77071-284-3 (softcover)
ISBN 978-1-77071-285-0 (multi-user eBook)

Printed in the United States of America in North Mankato, Minnesota
1 2 3 4 5 6 7 8 9 0   17 16 15 14 13

062013
WEP130613

We acknowledge the financial support of the Government of Canada through
the Canada Book Fund for our publishing activities.

Photograph and Text Credits
Library and Archives Canada: 3, 4, 5, 7, 10, 20, 21, 23, 27, 30
Getty Images: 5, 15, 17, 28
Alamy Images: 10–11, 13, 19, 23, 29

Every reasonable effort has been made to trace ownership and to obtain
permission to reprint copyright material. The publishers would be pleased
to have any errors or omissions brought to their attention so that they may
be corrected in subsequent printings.

Editor
Pamela Dell

Project Coordinator
Aaron Carr

Art Director
Terry Paulhus

CONTENTS

The Resistors

In 1867, the new nation of Canada began to expand west into the prairies. However, the **Métis** and First Nations already lived there. These peoples resisted Canada's expansion. They were led by Louis Riel, a Métis leader. Proud of his Métis roots and a powerful speaker, Riel made other Métis feel proud of their culture as well. His ability to speak for his people and his demand that they be heard made him a natural leader during the period of the North-West Resistance.

BIG BEAR

Mistahimaskwa, or Big Bear, was a famous chief of the Prairie River people. He tried to unite First Nations people in a **confederation** and became a leader among the Cree Nation. During the North-West Resistance, Big Bear tried to stop the fighting.

GABRIEL DUMONT

Gabriel Dumont was a Métis chief and warrior who grew up in the Red River Settlement. He became the military commander of the Métis during the North-West Resistance. In 1876, he started a Métis colony in what is now the province of Saskatchewan.

POUNDMAKER

Pitikwahanapiwiyin, or Poundmaker, was born among the Plains Cree in what is now Saskatchewan. Poundmaker became chief of one of the River People bands. He supported the Métis struggle, but he tried to bring peace during the North-West Resistance.

"I am more convinced every day that without a single exception I did right. And I have always believed that, as I have acted honestly, the time will come when the people of Canada will see and acknowledge it." Louis Riel

The Métis lived a rugged life of farming and hunting to survive.

Early Canada and the Métis

In 1534, French explorer Jacques Cartier arrived in what would become Quebec. British explorers soon followed. From this time on, France and Britain fought for control of the land and its natural resources. Fur traders and **settlers** were soon exploring the land, hunting and trapping animals such as beavers and bison. There were two companies the fur traders could work for. The British Hudson's Bay Company was one. The North West Company, which was French, was the other company.

The land was harsh, and the fur traders struggled to survive. They hired **Aboriginal** people as their guides. These First Nations people helped the fur traders survive and find their way through the wilderness. The traders built friendships with the First Nations people. Some French fur traders of the North West Company started families with First Nations women. These half-French, half-Aboriginal people built their own communities and culture. They became known as the Métis. Though a small group, the Métis would end up having a huge impact on Canada. Fighting for their rights in the North-West Resistance, they would change the country forever.

On June 1, 1821, the North West Company joined with the Hudson's Bay Company. Many fur-trading posts were closed, and the Métis were greatly affected by the decrease in the fur trade. This was only the beginning of their troubles.

When the Hudson's Bay Company took over the North West Company's land in 1821, it gained control of an area the size of Australia.

The North West Company hired French Canadians called *voyageurs* to transport fur and other goods by canoe. These voyageurs helped explore much of the country.

Confederation and Expansion

The Métis lived in an area called the Red River Settlement, where Winnipeg, Manitoba, is located today. They spoke French, hunted bison, and farmed. They loved the land in which they lived, and considered it their own.

Then, on July 1, 1867, Canada became an independent nation known as the **Dominion** of Canada. That same year, the United States bought the **territory** of Alaska. The American and Canadian governments had similar goals. The Americans sought control of western North America. John A. Macdonald, Canada's first prime minister, wanted to expand Canada to the west. Both governments sent settlers to claim land on the prairies. When English settlers from Canada and the United States arrived, the Métis feared they would lose their land, language, and culture.

A new trouble arose for the Métis when, after more than 200 years of fur trading, the Hudson's Bay Company decided to sell the vast area of land it owned, called **Rupert's Land**. It was just what the Canadian government needed. In 1869, the British **Crown** bought Rupert's Land and gave it to Canada.

Prime Minister Macdonald now had the land he wanted to bring about the expansion of Canada, but there was a problem. Métis and First Nations groups believed it was their land. They were not willing to hand it over to the Canadians.

LEGEND

	British Territory		Canada		Rupert's Land
	Newfoundland		United States		Unclaimed Land

JULY 1

1497–1759 1867 1869 1869–1870 1870 1870

Canada in 1867

Hudson Bay

Atlantic
Ocean

The Red River Rebellion

When a Canadian politician named William McDougall was sent to take control of Rupert's Land in November 1869, Louis Riel went to meet him. He stopped McDougall on November 2, before McDougall reached the Métis settlement on the Red River. "Go back to Ottawa and tell them that these are Métis lands," Riel said. "You are not welcome here!" McDougall left, but Riel knew the Canadians would be back.

On the same day, Riel and his supporters attacked Fort Garry, a Hudson's Bay trading post. They also formed a new government. One reason Riel created this government was to use it to **negotiate** with the Canadian government. Some pro-Canadian settlers fled the Red River settlement and went to Lower Fort Garry, 32 kilometres north on the Red River. The Red River Rebellion had begun.

"We consider it not asking too much to request that the government allow us to occupy our lands in peace."
Gabriel Dumont

Today, Lower Fort Garry is a national historic site near Selkirk, Manitoba.

A Deal and a Mistake

Back in Ottawa, the prime minister decided that Canada would not take over Rupert's Land until the Red River Rebellion ended. In December, he sent Donald Smith, an important figure in the Hudson's Bay Company, to negotiate with the Métis. Smith arrived on December 27, but did not meet with Riel until January 5, 1870. At this meeting, Louis Riel demanded that Canada recognize Métis rights, saying, "We are free and spirited, and we will not allow the Dominion of Canada to trample on our rights."

Smith had the authority to negotiate for the Canadian government. He told Riel that the Canadian government would let the Métis keep their land, language, and culture. The Red River Settlement would become part of Canada, and the Métis would be in charge of governing their own province.

Some English settlers did not agree. They tried to take Fort Garry back from the Métis. Riel arrested them. One of the men, Thomas Scott, threatened to shoot Riel. Riel ordered a trial, and Scott was found guilty of **treason** against the new government of Manitoba. He was sentenced to death. On March 4, 1870, Thomas Scott was shot and killed by a firing squad.

"[The Métis] must be kept down by a strong hand until they are swamped by the influx of settlers." Prime Minister John A. Macdonald

The city of Winnipeg was built over Fort Garry. Today, little of the original fort remains.

A New Province

Louis Riel was a hero to French Canadians, but English Canadians were angry because of Thomas Scott's killing. The deal between the government and the Métis became official on July 15, 1870. The Manitoba Act created the fifth Canadian province. The Métis now had their own province, which allowed them to keep their land, speak French, and continue their way of life. The Canadian government controlled the land that the Métis did not live on. Despite the Manitoba Act, more and more settlers continued to come to Manitoba looking for land.

The Manitoba Act also **pardoned** Louis Riel and the rest of the Métis for the Red River Rebellion. The government did not see them as criminals, but many English people in Canada did. They wanted Riel arrested for the murder of Thomas Scott. Riel was **exiled** from Canada. He moved to the United States, while Gabriel Dumont and other Métis went farther west into Saskatchewan where they started a **colony** at Batoche.

JULY 15

1497–1759 1867 1869 1869–1870 1870 1870

Before he left for the United States, Louis Riel gave his people advice. He said, "I have only this to say to the Métis, remain Métis, become more Métis than ever."

The Métis have made many contributions to Canada. One of their most famous was the Red River cart.

Broken Promises

In the United States, Riel became an American citizen and taught school in Montana. Back in the Canadian northwest, life was becoming difficult for First Nations people. The Canadian government wanted even more land, so they negotiated with the First Nations chiefs to create **treaties** all across the country. First Nations were promised land, food, and water. The Aboriginal people on the plains were very hungry. The bison they had hunted for thousands of years were nearly extinct. Big Bear, Poundmaker, and other chiefs signed the treaties because their people needed food.

Soon, the First Nations realized that the Canadian government was not keeping its promises. Thousands of First Nations people were starving to death, and they were being forced to move onto reserves. These reserves often lacked the supplies the First Nations needed to survive. They felt tricked by the government.

The Métis, as well as the settlers in Manitoba and the newly settled area of Saskatchewan, were also upset. The new Canadian Pacific Railway had reached the prairies. This railway was controlling the prices farmers had to pay to ship their crops to eastern Canada. The government was not helping. In 1884, a group went to the United States to bring Louis Riel to Batoche to help their cause.

When Europeans arrived in North America, at least 25 million bison roamed the great plains. By 1884, only a few thousand remained, many killed for sport.

Once hunted almost to extinction, bison have made a comeback. Today, there are more than 500,000 bison in North America.

Rebellion Reborn

In early July 1884, Louis Riel returned to Canada to lead the Métis, this time in Saskatchewan. He moved his family to Batoche, Saskatchewan. Things had changed since the Red River Rebellion of 1870. Back then, there had been no police in the Northwest. By 1884, the government of Canada had established the North-West Mounted Police (NWMP). They had forts all across the prairies and regularly patrolled the area, keeping the peace. Over the next eight months, tensions grew between the Métis and the government.

On March 18, 1885, Riel, Dumont, and a group of Métis were told that the NWMP were coming to arrest them. The group raided St. Anthony's church in Batoche and took control of the town. Just like he had done in Manitoba, Louis Riel now set up a Métis government in Saskatchewan.

Next, the Métis planned to take over a Hudson's Bay Company trading post at Fort Carlton. On their way, Dumont and his men stopped at the small community of Duck Lake to gather food and weapons. The NWMP arrived, which led to fighting on March 26. The Métis held their ground and the police force **retreated**. After 15 years of peace, the North-West Resistance had begun again.

1497–1759   1867   1869   1869–1870   1870   1870

"We left Manitoba because we were not free, and we came here to what was still a wild country in order to be free. And still they do not leave us alone." Gabriel Dumont

Today, St. Anthony's church is a popular tourist destination.

While the Métis were fighting, the First Nations were still starving on their reserves. The government had promised to give them food in return for staying out of the resistance. When the food never came, Poundmaker went to find it. He led a group of his people to the Saskatchewan town of Battleford. Seeing them coming and thinking they were being attacked, the townspeople fled. With no one to guard the supplies, some of the group decided to take what was there. Poundmaker tried to stop the people from stealing.

"These supplies do not belong to us," he said, but his people were too hungry to listen. Paying no attention, they took what they needed.

Big Bear's people were starving, too. The chief was a peaceful man, but some of his people decided to use violence to get what they needed. On April 2, 1885, a group of Big Bear's warriors attacked and killed nine settlers at the settlement of Frog Lake. Then, the warriors moved on to attack Fort Pitt for its food and other supplies. However, Big Bear convinced his people that violence was not necessary. The settlers left, and Big Bear's warriors captured Fort Pitt peacefully. Poundmaker and Big Bear had joined the resistance.

"Nothing is to be gained by killing the people of this fort. Let them go free." Big Bear

A great Blackfoot chief named Crowfoot adopted Poundmaker. The Cree and Blackfoot were enemies, but the adoption brought peace between the two nations.

On May 2, 1885, Poundmaker's camp was attacked by Canadian soldiers. Though outnumbered, the Cree fought off the soldiers.

Troop Transport

Prime Minister Macdonald wanted to end the North-West Resistance quickly. He knew that the longer it lasted, the more powerful the Métis would become. After the Duck Lake battle in March, he had sent the **militia** to lead the fight against them. Major-General Frederick Dobson Middleton was the commander of this Canadian militia. He was helped by Lieutenant-Colonel William Otter and almost 5,000 troops.

By this time, the Canadian Pacific Railway was nearly complete. This made it much easier for the government in Ottawa to move troops to the west. Within weeks, Middleton and his militia had arrived on the prairies. They joined the soldiers and NWMP who were already in Saskatchewan and others from Alberta. The militia was strong, but so was the resistance.

 The Canadian Pacific Railway was built between 1881 and 1885. It linked the entire country, helping unite Canada from east to west.

It took workers about two years to extend the Canadian Pacific Railway through the Rocky Mountains.

Gaining Strength

Middleton's intention was to march 900 troops directly to the Métis community of Batoche, Louis Riel's headquarters. Middleton planned to attack the Métis at their base. If he succeeded, it would end the fighting.

Knowing they were coming, however, Gabriel Dumont gathered 150 Métis and First Nations fighters. They hid in the trees along the banks of Fish Creek. The Métis and First Nations warriors were outnumbered, but they were fierce fighters. On April 24, they ambushed the Canadian militia. After more than six hours of fighting, Middleton and his troops retreated.

The resistance was gaining strength. Defeating the Canadian militia at Fish Creek gave the rebels hope, but Riel knew that Middleton and Otter would not give up. He decided to prepare for battle at Batoche.

STANDING THEIR GROUND
On May 2, 1885, Lt. Col. Otter and 325 troops attacked Poundmaker's camp. They marched more than 50 kilometres through freezing rain to reach a hill above the Cut Knife Reserve. Again, the First Nations fighters hid in the trees and fired on the militia. Otter had bigger guns and more men, but the Cree warriors were excellent fighters. The militia retreated.

1497–1759   1867   1869   1869–1870   1870   1870

"In a little while it will be over. We may fail. But the rights for which we contend will not die." Louis Riel

In the Battle of Fish Creek, 16 people were killed, including four Métis. About 45 people were wounded.

On May 9, Middleton arrived at Batoche with several hundred troops. The Métis and First Nations only had a few hundred people, but they managed to hold off the government militia for three days.

Middleton tried to outsmart the Métis, but Dumont was an intelligent leader. Early on, Middleton ordered a steamboat to sail down the river and attack the Métis forces from behind. Dumont's men lowered a ferry cable across the river, and when the boat hit the cable, its smokestacks were cut off. Without power, the steamboat drifted, unable to move forward.

On May 12, Middleton ordered a new attack. A small group went in from one side to draw Dumont's men out into the open. A second group had been ordered to attack from the opposite side when they heard the gunfire. They waited, but it was so windy they failed to hear the guns. The second attack never came. Middleton was angry. His plan had failed, but after a three-day battle, the resistance fighters were running out of bullets.

RETREAT AND SURRENDER
Dumont ran to freedom in the United States. Riel surrendered. Poundmaker and Big Bear knew that without the Métis' help, the First Nations could not win. They surrendered as well. The North-West Resistance was over. Canada had won.

1497–1759   1867   1869   1869–1870   1870   1870

After his arrest, Riel wrote poetry in his jail cell. "Is there any one to side / With me? Yes. Sincerity / Will gather up its recruits. / And we will soon taste its fruits."

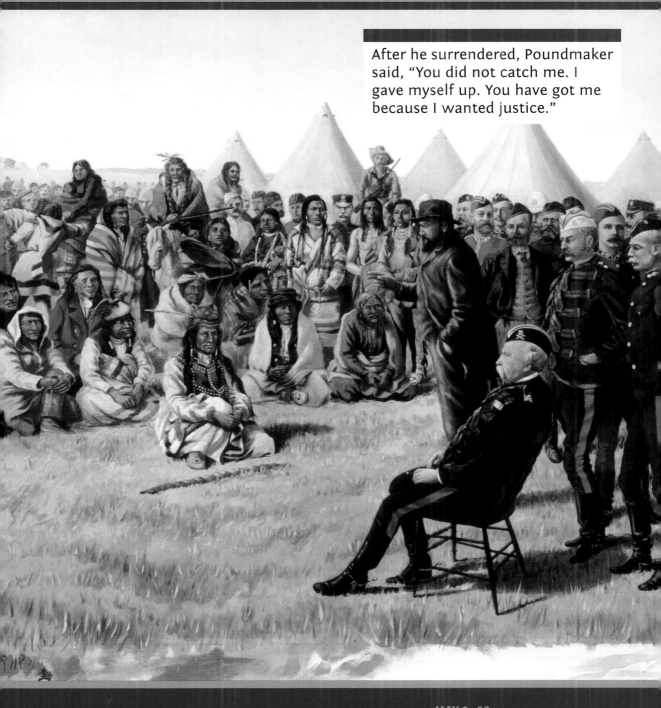

After he surrendered, Poundmaker said, "You did not catch me. I gave myself up. You have got me because I wanted justice."

A Hero Lives On

Louis Riel surrendered on May 15, 1885. Soon after, Poundmaker and Big Bear also surrendered. They, along with many other prisoners, were taken to Regina, Saskatchewan, for trial. Poundmaker and Big Bear were sentenced to three years in prison. On August 3, Louis Riel was found guilty of treason and sentenced to death.

After his trial, Riel said, "Deeds are not accomplished in a few days or in a few hours. A century is only a spoke in the wheel of everlasting time." On November 16, Louis Riel was hanged. The actions of Riel and his supporters resulted in many changes in Canada. The North-West Resistance led to the creation of two new Canadian provinces, Manitoba and Saskatchewan.

In 2003, more than 100 years after Riel's death, the Métis were recognized by the Canadian government as an Aboriginal People. They were given rights to their own customs and traditional lands. More than 250,000 Métis live in Canada today.

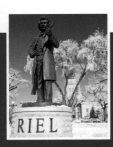

RIEL

A HERO IS MADE
Louis Riel is considered a hero across Canada. Louis Riel Day is celebrated every year on the third Monday of February.

1497–1759   1867   1869   1869–1870   1870   1870

"We must cherish our inheritance. We must preserve our nationality for the youth of our future. The story should be written down to pass on." Louis Riel

Today, there are many monuments to Louis Riel in Manitoba.

Brain Teaser

1. What was the name of the French fur trading company?

2. When did Canada become an independent country?

3. Who were the Métis?

4. Why did Louis Riel establish a new government in Manitoba in 1869?

5. What was the outcome of the Red River Rebellion of 1869 to 1870?

6. Who was Big Bear?

7. In what year were the Métis finally recognized as an Aboriginal people by the government of Canada?

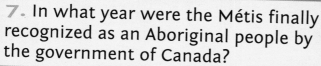

7. 2003

6. Big Bear was a Cree leader who fought during the North-West Resistance. He wanted peace and justice for his people.

5. The Red River Rebellion resulted in the formation of the province of Manitoba. It also ended with Riel's exile to the United States.

4. He started a government so he could use it to help him negotiate with the Canadian government.

3. The Métis were the descendants of French traders and First Nations peoples.

2. 1867

1. The North West Company

ANSWERS

Further Information

See the history of Canada unfold at *www.collectionscanada.gc.ca/confederation/kids/023002-1000-e.html*

Check out this map to learn more about the fur trade *www.canadiangeographic.ca/atlas/themes.aspx?id=furtrade&lang=En*

Learn more about the Métis at *www.collectionscanada.gc.ca/settlement/kids/021013-2081-e.html*

Watch this video about the North-West Resistance *www.youtube.com/watch?v=JvxKHSXjnZ8*

Read all about Louis Riel at *www.collectionscanada.gc.ca/confederation/023001-4000.61-e.html*

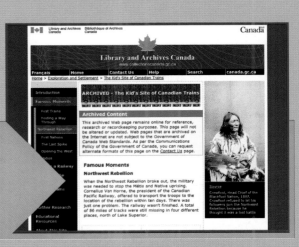

Learn more about how the Canadian Pacific Railway helped end the North-West Resistance *www.collectionscanada.gc.ca/trains/kids/021007-1030-e.html*

Glossary

Aboriginal: the original inhabitants of an area

colony: foreign land settled by the people of a nation

confederation: an organization made up of many groups joined in an alliance

Crown: the reigning monarch of country; represents the government of a country

dominion: an independent nation within the British Empire

executed: to be killed as a punishment for a crime

exiled: forced to leave one's country

Métis: a person of mixed Aboriginal and European descent

militia: a body of citizens with some military training who are called to active duty only in an emergency

negotiate: to try and reach an agreement between different groups

pardoned: forgiven for a crime

retreated: pulled back from a battle

Rupert's Land: nearly 4 million square kilometres of land located between Labrador and the Rocky Mountains

settlers: people who move to a new land to make new lives there

territory: an area of land

treason: a crime considered to betray one's country; often involves trying to overthrow the government

treaties: written agreements

Index